MIKAEL KROGERUS
ROMAN TSCHÄPPELER

THE QUESTION BOOK

**WHO ARE YOU?
532 OPPORTUNITIES FOR
SELF-REFLECTION AND DISCOVERY**

Translated from the German by Jamie Lee Searle

**Also by Mikael Krogerus & Roman Tschäppeler
and available from Profile Books:**

The Change Book
The Collaboration Book
The Decision Book
The Get Things Done Book
The Test Book

CONTENTS

Operating instructions 1
The last year 2
Right now 8
Rituals and routines 13
Vices 17
Talking and writing 19
How you work 21
What your boss thinks of you 28
Mind and body 30
House and home 38
Take three 44
Confessions 48
Money and possessions 50
Who you are 56
Who you *really* are 62
Principles and values 67
Politics and opinions 70
Eco and bio 76
The first time and the last time 80
Travel 82
Childhood memories 87
Your family 90
You and your siblings 96
What your parents think of you 98
Love 100
What your partner thinks of you 110
Being single 112
Sex 114
Your friendships 118
What your friends think of you 124
Your future 126

Making decisions	129
Thinking about having children	132
Being a parent	135
On happiness	139
A question of faith	142
Your fears	147
Dying	150
Final questions	153
Your questions	159
Any more questions?	169
Acknowledgements	170
About the authors	171

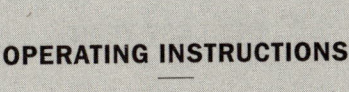

OPERATING INSTRUCTIONS

You can complete *The Question Book* while you're alone, like a diary. You can use it to make a long train journey pass in the blink of an eye, or as a guide for writing your memoir. *The Question Book* can be used to enliven a boring dinner party, or to draw relatives out of their shell. You can bring excitement back into your relationship, or finally get to know your parents. It will help you engage your children in conversation, or get the most taciturn of men to talk. You can work through the book from cover to cover; or open it at a random page; or pick a number between 1 and 532 – and ask the corresponding question. Not every question will apply to every person, and not every label will either – feel free to scribble on the pages, cross things out and add more questions (there's a space at the back to do this!). This book is for you – make it your own.

We believe everyone has a story to tell; you just need to ask the right question.

Four rules of play
1. Don't overthink it; go with whatever answer comes to mind.
2. There are no right answers, only honest ones.
3. Any answer is valid until you amend it.
4. We all admire people who give good answers. And we admire even more those who ask good questions. But best of all are the people who genuinely listen.

THE LAST YEAR

Think back on the past twelve months.

No. 1 Your book of the year:

No. 2 Your song of the year:

No. 3 Your film of the year:

No. 4 The item of clothing you most enjoyed wearing:

No. 5 The best sex:

No. 6 The most important person:

No. 7 The most annoying person:

THE LAST YEAR

No. 8 Someone you apologised to:

No. 9 Someone you got to know:

No. 10 Someone you lost or left:

No. 11 Someone you neglected:

Someone who neglected you:

No. 12 A big argument:

No. 13 Which friend did you see most frequently?

THE LAST YEAR

No. 14 Who inspired you?

Who did you inspire?

No. 15 Something that changed your life:

No. 16 What present made you happiest?

No. 17 An expensive purchase:

No. 18 A plan that you carried out:

No. 19 The best trip:

No. 20 A (professional) success:

No. 21 A big disappointment:

No. 22 Have you earned more or less this year than the year before?
[ ] more [ ] less

No. 23 Something you did differently this year to the year before?

No. 24 How often were you ill?

No. 25 What were you grateful for?

No. 26 Something you learned to do:

Something you forgot how to do:

THE LAST YEAR

No. 27 The political or global incident that most affected you:

No. 28 The most fun party of the year:

No. 29 Three words that sum up your year:

No. 30 A new habit:

No. 31 Your guilty pleasure:

No. 32 Something that surprised you:

No. 33 The most difficult decision:

THE LAST YEAR

No. 34 Something you regret doing:

No. 35 Something you regret not doing:

No. 36 Has this past year been your best yet?

Why, or why not?

RIGHT NOW

No. 37 Where are you right now?

....

....

....

....

No. 38 Two things you've done today:

1. ....

2. ....

No. 39 Two people you've been thinking about a lot recently:

1. ....

2. ....

RIGHT NOW

No. 40 A word that describes ...

- your health: ....
- your financial situation: ....
- your work: ....
- your sex life: ....
- your relationships: ....
- your life: ....

No. 41 A newspaper or website that you read regularly:

....

No. 42 Your favourite shoes:

....

No. 43 Your perfume:

....

RIGHT NOW

No. 44 A sport you enjoy doing:

....

• A sport you enjoy watching: ....

No. 45 Your favourite toy

• In the past: ....

• Now: ....

No. 46 What languages do you speak?

• Fluently: ....

• Well: ....

No. 47 What language would you like to speak?

....

No. 48 How many days a week do you drink alcohol?

[ ] never   [ ] 1–3 x   [ ] 4–6 x   [ ] every day

No. 49 When do you not drink alcohol?

   ....

No. 50 Two recipes you know by heart:

   1. ....

   2. ....

No. 51 A recipe you've mastered which is always well received:

   ....

No. 52 Roughly how much do you spend on food each month?

   • For cooking at home: ....

   • Eating out : ....

No. 53 Which foods do you spend a lot of money on?

   ....

No. 54   Which foods do you prefer to save money on?

   ....

No. 55   A programme you watch regularly:

   ....

No. 56   The most famous person you've ever spoken to:

   ....

No. 57   What's your nickname?

   ....

   • Who calls you that? ....

RITUALS AND ROUTINES

No. 58   What time do you usually go to bed?

[ ] a.m.

[ ] p.m.

No. 59   What time do you usually get up?

[ ] a.m.

[ ] p.m.

No. 60   What is your favourite time of day?

[ ] a.m.

[ ] p.m.

- Why? ....

No. 61   The position you fall asleep in:

[ ]   [ ]

[ ]   [ ]

No. 62   Do you have a tic or neurosis?

....

No. 63   What do you usually do when you need to think something over?

....

....

RITUALS AND ROUTINES

No. 64 What do you wear when you want to look your best?

....

....

No. 65 Describe a perfect day:

....

....

No. 66 Describe a daily ritual that means a lot to you:

....

....

No. 67 A lovely ritual from your childhood:

....

....

No. 68 What ritual would you like to introduce to your life?

....

....

RITUALS AND ROUTINES

No. 69 What rituals have you given up?

....

....

No. 70 Which rituals in other people do you find ridiculous?

....

....

No. 71 What new belief or habit has most improved your life over the last five years?

....

....

VICES

No. 72 An alcoholic drink you often order:

....

No. 73 A favourite drink from your youth:

....

No. 74 Your favourite bar:

....

- Why? ....

No. 75 Your worst experience with drugs:

....

- Your best experience with drugs:

....

VICES

No. 76 Something you're addicted to:

....

• Are you okay with this, or would you like to stop?

[ ] I'm okay with it   [ ] I'd like to stop

No. 77 Something you used to be addicted to, but no longer are:

....

• How did you manage to quit?

....

....

No. 78 How do you reward yourself?

....

No. 79 What is your worst habit?

....

TALKING AND WRITING

No. 80   On the chart below, plot how you tend to talk about:

- Your workday (A)
- Your relationship (D)
- Your holidays (B)
- Your sex life (E)
- Your successes (C)
- Your problems (F)

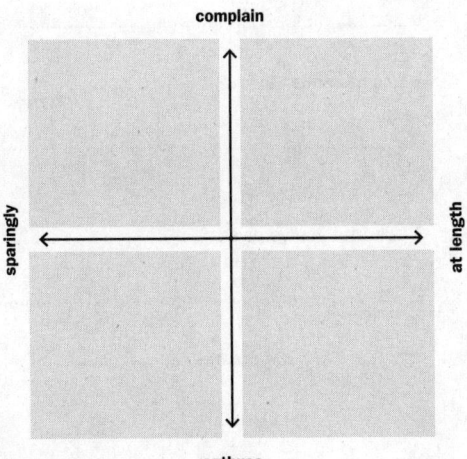

TALKING AND WRITING

No. 81 Two words, phrases or expressions that you use frequently:

1. ....

2. ....

No. 82 Do you express yourself better when talking or writing?

[ ] talking   [ ] writing

No. 83 Who have you written to recently?

....

• Who has written to you?

....

No. 84 A talk that you've given:

....

....

HOW YOU WORK

No. 85 What do you do for a living?

....

No. 86 When you were younger, what did you want to do for a living?

....

- Did you choose to do that? Why or why not?

....

....

No. 87 What did your parents want you to do for a living?

....

- Did you choose to do that? Why or why not?

....

....

No. 88   What other career would be a good fit for you?

....

....

No. 89   Besides your current career, what are you so good at that someone would pay you to do it?

....

....

No. 90   What work would you do if you didn't need to earn money?

....

....

No. 91   Do you have a career role model?

....

No. 92   Who would you ask to write a reference for you?

....

....

HOW YOU WORK

No. 93 Describe a turning point in your existing career:

....

....

No. 94 Who do you compete with? Which of you is in the lead?

....

....

No. 95 What has been your biggest professional defeat? What did you learn from it?

....

....

No. 96 What is your most important characteristic in terms of your work?

....

No. 97 Would you prefer to have more or less responsibility at work?

[ ] more   [ ] less   [ ] the same

No. 98 How under-challenged or overextended do you feel?
        Draw a cross on the line below:

        under-challenged ⟵——————⟶ overextended

No. 99 Do you get on well with your work colleagues?

        [ ] yes   [ ] no

        • Why do you think this might be?

        ....

        ....

No. 100 What are your superiors doing wrong?

        ....

        ....

No. 101 Do you work better alone or as part of a team?
        Draw a cross on the line below:

        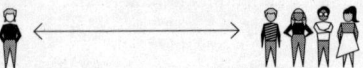

No. 102 Have you ever been unemployed? If so:

- How did it happen?

....

....

- How did you cope with it?

....

....

No. 103 Do you do any voluntary work?

[ ] yes   [ ] no

- If yes, why?

....

....

- If no, why not?

....

....

No. 104 Plot all the paid jobs you've ever had on the chart.

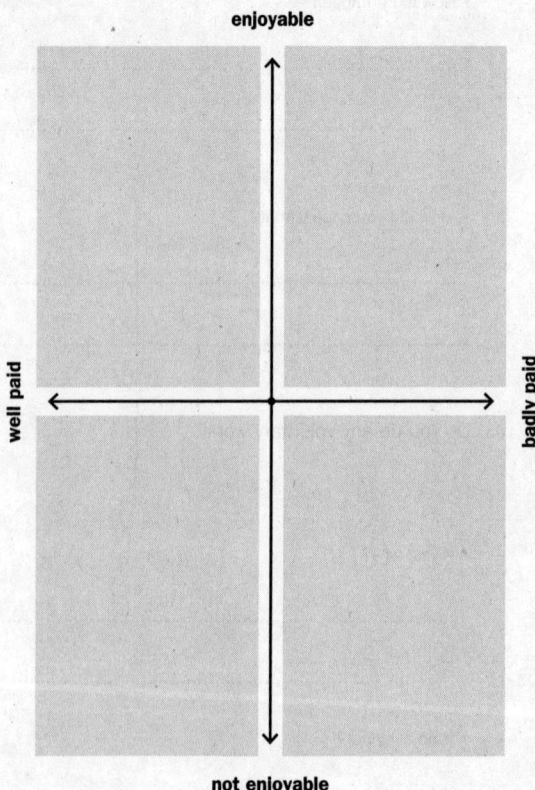

HOW YOU WORK

No. 105 If you are retired, are you happy about it?

....

- Do you feel anything is missing? If so, what?

....

....

No. 106 What's your coping mechanism when you feel uncertain in a professional situation?

....

....

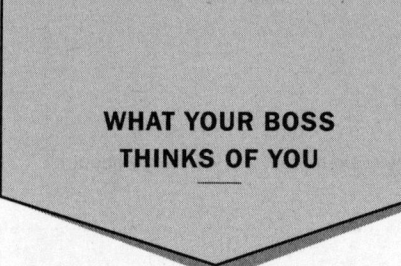

WHAT YOUR BOSS THINKS OF YOU

Ask your manager!
> If you can't ask them – or would prefer not to – then put yourself in their shoes and ask yourself: what would they say?

Name of your boss: ....

No. 107 Three things I'm good at:

1. ....

2. ....

3. ....

No. 108 How predictable am I? Draw a cross on the line below:

unpredictable ⟵——————⟶ predictable

No. 109 How important am I to the company? Draw a cross on the line below:

unimportant ⟵———————————————⟶ important

No. 110 Do I earn too much, too little, or the right amount? Why?

....

....

....

No. 111 How popular am I with my colleagues? Why?

....

....

....

No. 112 Something I should change:

....

....

....

MIND AND BODY

No. 113 How many hours of sleep do you need?

....

• How many hours of sleep do you get?

....

No. 114 Your strategy when you can't get to sleep:

....

No. 115 Your recipe for relaxation:

....

No. 116 Would you like to be ...

    [ ] slimmer   [ ] stronger

    [ ] more flexible   [ ] more energetic

MIND AND BODY

No. 117 Do you exercise?

[ ] yes   [ ] no

- How many times a week? ....

- What do you like about the exercise you do?

....

....

- Do you feel you should exercise more? If so, why?

....

....

No. 118 What has been your greatest sporting achievement?

....

....

No. 119 Which sport would you like to be good at?

....

No. 120 Mark on the pictures ...

- two of your problem zones.

- two features you are proud of.

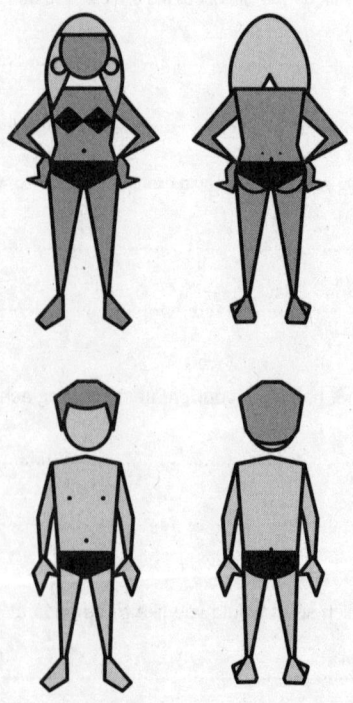

MIND AND BODY

No. 121 Mark on the pictures ...

- three things you like about your partner's body.

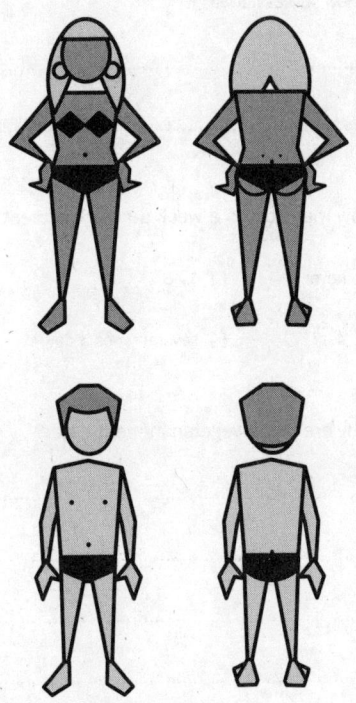

No. 122 Have you ever been on a diet?

- If yes, what kind?

....

- How successful was it?

....

....

No. 123 How many times a week do you eat meat?

[ ] never   [ ] 1–3

[ ] 4–7   [ ] several times a day

No. 124 Why are you a vegetarian/meat eater?

....

....

....

....

....

MIND AND BODY

No. 125 Which type of medicine(s) do you take regularly?

....

- Which medicine(s) do you think you should take?

....

- Which medicine(s) do you think you should *stop* taking?

....

No. 126 What phobias do you have?

....

No. 127 How stressed do you feel? Draw a cross on the line below:

relaxed ⟵——————————⟶ burnt-out

No. 128 What helps you when you're stressed?

....

....

....

MIND AND BODY

No. 129 Your worst experience of illness:

....

....

No. 130 Your worst accident:

....

....

No. 131 Fill in the table below. What is the worst pain you've ever ... experienced? ... inflicted on someone else?

	experienced	inflicted on someone else
emotional		
physical		

No. 132 What medical condition do you imagine to be so unbearable that you would consider ending your life?

....

• Why?

....

....

No. 133 What age would you like to live to?

....

No. 134 Have you ever been in psychotherapy?

[ ] yes   [ ] no

• If yes, why? ....

• If no, why not? ....

HOUSE AND HOME

No. 135 How old were you when you left home?

....

No. 136 Do you prefer to live alone, or with someone? Explain your answer.

....

....

....

No. 137 Think back on everyone you've ever lived with ...

• Who did it work best with?

....

• Who did it really not work with?

....

No. 138 Sketch the floorplan of the first place you lived after leaving home.

HOUSE AND HOME

No. 139 Which of your friends can you imagine living with?

....

No. 140 How much of your income goes on your rent or mortgage?

.... %

No. 141 What is the nicest apartment or house you ever lived in?

- Address: ....

....

....

- What is the nicest location you've lived in?

....

No. 142 What is your favourite street? Would you like to live there?

....

....

HOUSE AND HOME

No. 143 What's your favourite spot in your home?

....

No. 144 Two things you like about your home:

1. ....

2. ....

No. 145 Two things you don't like about your home:

1. ....

2. ....

No. 146 Describe your dream apartment/house:

....

....

....

....

....

....

HOUSE AND HOME

No. 147 How do you envision your ideal lifestyle after retirement?

....

....

No. 148 Where do you feel at home?

....

No. 149 How chaotic or organised are you? Draw a cross on the line below:

chaotic ⟵─────────────⟶ organised

- Would you like to be different?

[ ] yes   [ ] no

- What's stopping you?

....

No. 150 How many times a year do you receive reminders for unpaid bills?

....

HOUSE AND HOME

No. 151 Your household. Do you: yes   no

- always clean up the kitchen immediately?   [ ]   [ ]
- do the vacuuming every week?   [ ]   [ ]
- have a cleaner?   [ ]   [ ]
- iron your clothes?   [ ]   [ ]
- take off your shoes when you enter someone's home?   [ ]   [ ]
- ask your guests to take off their shoes when they enter your home?   [ ]   [ ]
- replace the toilet roll as soon as you finish it?   [ ]   [ ]
- do the laundry?   [ ]   [ ]
- do the weekly shop?   [ ]   [ ]

TAKE THREE

No. 152 Three places you've lived:

1.
2.
3.

No. 153 Three books you love:

1.
2.
3.

No. 154 Three films you'd watch again:

1.
2.
3.

No. 155 Three TV series where you've seen every episode:

1.
2.
3.

No. 156 Three apps you'd most recommend:

1.
2.
3.

No. 157 Look at your music app. What are the last three songs you played?

1.
2.
3.

• What are your three most frequently played songs?

1.
2.
3.

No. 158 Three games you enjoy playing:

1.
2.
3.

No. 159 Your top three drinks:
1.
2.
3.

No. 160 Your top three brands:
1.
2.
3.

No. 161 Three favourite restaurants:
1.
2.
3.

No. 162 Three tasks that annoy you:
1.
2.
3.

TAKE THREE

No. 163 Three things that annoy you about other people:

1.
2.
3.

No. 164 Three topics you like talking about:

1.
2.
3.

No. 165 Three shops you like to buy from:

1.
2.
3.

No. 166 Three things you do when you're bored:

1.
2.
3.

CONFESSIONS

No. 167 A film that really scared you:

· And one that made you cry:

No. 168 Something you have absolutely no idea about:

No. 169 Something that you spend too much money on:

No. 170 Something that makes you happy:

No. 171 Something that bores you:

No. 172 Something you never want to do again:

CONFESSIONS

No. 173   Something you consider sacred:

No. 174   Music you like, but would rather not admit you listen to:

No. 175   The best gig or concert you've ever been to:

No. 176   A piece of art that makes you feel incredibly calm:

No. 177   Describe an experience in nature that moved you:

MONEY AND POSSESSIONS

No. 178 Your approximate bank balance:

    Account 1:
    Account 2:
    Account 3:
    Other accounts:
    Total:

No. 179 Your monthly income:

....

No. 180 Could you get by with less money?

    [ ] yes   [ ] no

No. 181 Could you get by with half of your current income?

    [ ] yes   [ ] no

MONEY AND POSSESSIONS

No. 182 How much do you earn compared with your best friends?

[ ] more [ ] less [ ] roughly the same

No. 183 You earn ...

[ ] too much [ ] too little [ ] just the right amount

No. 184 To whom do you owe money?

....

....

No. 185 Who owes you money?

....

....

No. 186 Have you ever stolen anything?

[ ] yes [ ] no

• If yes, what was it?

....

MONEY AND POSSESSIONS

No. 187 Have you ever evaded paying taxes?

[ ] yes [ ] no [ ] don't know

No. 188 Which three things (not people) would you rescue if your apartment/house was on fire?

1. ....

2. ....

3. ....

No. 189 Something that you've owned since childhood:

....

No. 190 Something that you've thrown away or lost and wish you could have back:

....

....

No. 191 Something you ought to part with:

....

....

MONEY AND POSSESSIONS

No. 192 Something you would buy yourself now if you could afford it:

....

No. 193 Do you play the lottery?

[ ] yes [ ] no [ ] occasionally

No. 194 Do you own stocks and shares?

[ ] yes [ ] no

• If so, since when? ....

No. 195 Have you ever experienced financial trouble?

[ ] yes [ ] no

• If yes, why?

....

• What did you do about it?

....

....

MONEY AND POSSESSIONS

No. 196 Which of your friends know how much you earn?

....

No. 197 If you have a partner, do you have a shared bank account?

[ ] yes   [ ] no

No. 198 Are you open and transparent with your partner about your finances?

....

....

....

....

No. 199 How much money would you leave behind if you died tomorrow?

....

....

....

MONEY AND POSSESSIONS 55

No. 200 Write down five valuable things that you own, placing them on the graph according to both their monetary and sentimental value.

WHO YOU ARE

No. 201 What is your nationality? If you have more than one nationality, list them all.

....

- What common stereotypes do people have about your nationality?

....

- Which of these stereotypes apply to you?

....

No. 202 Two people who have influenced you:

1. ....

2. ....

No. 203 Two events that have influenced you:

1. ....

2. ....

WHO YOU ARE

No. 204 Your two best character traits:

1. ....

2. ....

No. 205 Your two worst character traits:

1. ....

2. ....

No. 206 Two compliments you often receive:

1. ....

2. ....

- Which means more to you?

[ ] 1   [ ] 2

No. 207 Something hurtful that was once said to you:

....

....

....

....

No. 208 What is a sign of independence?

....

• Do you feel independent?   [ ] yes   [ ] no

No. 209 Do you think you act appropriately for your age?

[ ] yes   [ ] no

• Yes, because ....

• No, because ....

No. 210 A significant change in your life over the last two years:

....

No. 211 What aggravates you?

....

No. 212 What have you struggled with in the past, but have now learned to live with?

....

....

No. 213 A behavioural pattern that you would like to get rid of:

....

....

- Why haven't you managed to get rid of it?

....

....

No. 214 An experience that you tell people about again and again:

....

....

No. 215 Something you should really keep quiet about:

....

....

No. 216 What do you think you spend ...

- too much time on? ....

- too little time on? ....

No. 217 Two activities you continue to do, even though you think they're pointless:

1. ....

2. ....

No. 218 Two things you regret:

1. ....

2. ....

No. 219 Two things you're proud of:

1. ....

2. ....

No. 220 Which question was easier for you to answer?

[ ] No. 218   [ ] No. 219

No. 221 What makes you cry?

....

....

No. 222 In the space below, write the names of your closest relatives, then map out your relationship to each of them using a solid, broken, or dotted line.

WHO YOU *REALLY* ARE

No. 223 Are you more pessimistic or optimistic?

[ ] pessimistic   [ ] optimistic

• Why do you think this is?

....

....

No. 224 Describe a situation in which you felt overwhelmed:

....

....

....

No. 225 Describe a situation in which you felt unsure:

....

....

No. 226 Draw a cross on the line below to show how loyal you are:

disloyal ⟵—————————⟶ loyal

No. 227 Draw a cross on the line below to show how reliable you are:

unreliable ⟵—————————⟶ reliable

- A moment when you were unreliable:

....

No. 228 Draw a cross on the line below to show how brave you are:

cowardly ⟵—————————⟶ brave

- A moment when you were brave:

....
....

- A moment when you were cowardly:

....
....

No. 229 Three skills you would like to have:

1. ....

2. ....

3. ....

No. 230 Which of the following attributes are you most in need of right now?

[ ] persistence   [ ] imagination   [ ] courage   [ ] calm

No. 231 What do you think you are better at than most of your friends?

....

....

No. 232 When you receive a compliment, are you usually pleased and accept it, or do you feel that you haven't earned it?

....

- Explain why: ....

....

No. 233 Draw a cross on the line below to show whether, in your relationships, your partner usually loves you more than you love them – or vice versa:

receive love ←————————————————→ give love

No. 234 In conversations with friends, do you talk more or listen more? Draw a cross on the line below:

talk ←————————————————→ listen

No. 235 What is your reputation among your friends?

....

....

No. 236 Who are you in competition with?

....

....

No. 237 What impact do you think you have on others?

....

....

No. 238 Would you like to have yourself as a friend?

[ ] yes [ ] no

No. 239 Can you handle losing?

[ ] yes [ ] no

No. 240 Do you mind if someone does not like you? Expand on your answer.

....

....

....

No. 241 Have you ever hit your partner?

[ ] yes [ ] no

- Your children? [ ] yes [ ] no

- If yes to either, what were the circumstances?

....

....

PRINCIPLES AND VALUES

No. 242 Name a trivial criminal offence you've committed:

....

....

No. 243 How would you define moral courage, and when did you last demonstrate it?

....

....

....

No. 244 What virtue do you consider to be overrated? Give a reason.

....

....

....

PRINCIPLES AND VALUES

No. 245 Have you ever read your partner's diary or text messages?

[ ] yes   [ ] no

• If yes, does your partner know about it?

[ ] yes   [ ] no

• What did you discover?

....

• Do you regret the discovery?

....

No. 246 When did you last tell a lie?

....

....

No. 247 What are you deceiving yourself about?

....

....

....

PRINCIPLES AND VALUES

No. 248 If you found out that the child you were expecting was certain to be born with a disability, how would you react?

....

....

....

• How do you think your partner would react?

....

....

....

No. 249 What do you think has been the most important invention or achievement in the last fifty years?

....

....

• In the last twenty years?

....

....

POLITICS AND OPINIONS

No. 250 Are you for or against:

	for	against	don't know
• the tightening of asylum laws:	[ ]	[ ]	[ ]
• a divided Jerusalem:	[ ]	[ ]	[ ]
• the state bailing out banks:	[ ]	[ ]	[ ]
• the decriminalisation of sex work:	[ ]	[ ]	[ ]
• the abolition of animal testing:	[ ]	[ ]	[ ]
• the legalisation of cannabis:	[ ]	[ ]	[ ]
• limiting flights to two per person per year:	[ ]	[ ]	[ ]
• the death penalty:	[ ]	[ ]	[ ]

POLITICS AND OPINIONS

No. 251 What different communities are there in your local area?

....

• What is your relationship to the communities you don't belong to?

....

....

• How are your views on them influenced by stereotypes or prejudices?

....

....

....

No. 252 What do you think are the three most significant political events that have occurred during your lifetime?

1. ....

2. ....

3. ....

POLITICS AND OPINIONS

No. 253 Where were you when you heard the announcement of the first Coronavirus lockdown?

....

• What was your initial reaction?

....

....

No. 254 The two most urgent political topics:

1. ....

2. ....

• What have you done in support of them, or against them?

1. ....

2. ....

• What would make you do something?

1. ....

2. ....

POLITICS AND OPINIONS

No. 255 Where would you attack the system if you wanted to destroy it?

....

....

No. 256 Would you rather change the system or yourself?

[ ] system [ ] myself

No. 257 Do you think richer countries should send aid to less-developed countries?

[ ] yes [ ] no

• Why?

....

....

No. 258 Which political topic would you like to know more about?

....

....

POLITICS AND OPINIONS

No. 259 Are you a member of a political party? [ ] yes [ ] no

- If not, which political party would you be most likely to join?

....

No. 260 What would make you take to the streets in protest?

....

....

....

No. 261 When did you last vote?

....

- For what/whom did you last vote?

....

No. 262 Which politicians fill you with confidence?

....

....

....

POLITICS AND OPINIONS

No. 263 To what extent are you patriotic, and how do you show it?

....

....

....

....

No. 264 If you could introduce a new law in your country, what would it be?

....

....

....

....

ECO AND BIO

No. 265 Do you recycle?

[ ] yes   [ ] no

No. 266 Do you use fabric softener?

[ ] yes   [ ] no

No. 267 Approximately what percentage of your groceries are organic?

.... %

• Is this a priority for you?

....

• Why or why not?

....

....

....

No. 268 What risks related to food products most concern you?

[ ] pesticides, toxins, viruses

[ ] food additives

[ ] lacking vitamins and minerals

[ ] weight gain

[ ] animal welfare

[ ] environmental destruction

[ ] social inequality

[ ] ....

No. 269 If there are some products whose origins and manufacture don't bother you, which are they?

....

....

....

....

....

No. 270 If you drive a car:

• Which make is it, and why did you choose this one?

....

....

• What is its fuel consumption in litres per 100km or miles per gallon?

....

No. 271 What would you be prepared to do in order to reduce your CO_2 emissions?

[ ] give up your car

[ ] switch to eco-power

[ ] give up meat

[ ] move to a smaller house/apartment

[ ] stop travelling by plane

[ ] buy second-hand clothes

[ ] give up streaming services

[ ] ....

No. 272 Which environmental topic do you think is the most urgent?

....

....

- What have you done about it?

....

- If nothing, why not?

....

- What would make you do something about it?

....

No. 273 What luxury could you do without?

....

....

- Why don't you?

....

....

THE FIRST TIME AND THE LAST TIME

	the first time
No. 274 You were in love	
No. 275 You broke up with someone	
No. 276 Someone broke up with you	
No. 277 You cheated on someone	
No. 278 Someone cheated on you	
No. 279 You were drunk	
No. 280 You had sex	
No. 281 You travelled alone	
No. 282 You were the best at something	
No. 283 You lived alone	
No. 284 You took drugs	
No. 285 You thought about dying	

THE FIRST TIME AND THE LAST TIME

the last time

TRAVEL

No. 286 Do you usually pack too much, too little, or too late?

[ ] too much   [ ] too little   [ ] too late

No. 287 List three people you've met while travelling:

• Are you still in contact with them?

.... [ ] still in contact

.... [ ] still in contact

.... [ ] still in contact

No. 288 A person you fell in love with while travelling:

....

No. 289 Who would you travel the world with?

....

TRAVEL

No. 290 A dream travel destination from your childhood:

....

- Have you been? How was it?

....

....

....

....

....

No. 291 A trip that changed you:

....

....

....

....

....

....

No. 292 Enter the locations directly onto the maps.

- Your best trip ever (A)

- The last place you visited (B)

- Your next trip (C)

- A destination that disappointed you (D)

- Somewhere you would like to go (E)
  What would you like to see there?

....

TRAVEL

No. 293 Best and worst ...

- Best hotel: ....
- Most beautiful beach: ....
- Best restaurant: ....
- Most unfriendly country: ....
- Most friendly country: ....
- Worst travel experience: ....

No. 294 What do you miss when you're travelling?

....

....

No. 295 Where should everybody go once in their lifetime? Why?

....

No. 296 Which country, besides your own, do you know the most about?

....

CHILDHOOD MEMORIES

No. 297 Your first memory:

....

No. 298 A good childhood memory:

....

No. 299 A smell from your childhood:

....

No. 300 A word that describes your schooldays:

....

No. 301 Who was your favourite teacher, and what did you like about them?

....

CHILDHOOD MEMORIES

No. 302 What kind of economic background do you come from?

[ ] poor [ ] lower middle class

[ ] upper middle class [ ] wealthy

No. 303 How often did you move house during your childhood?

....

....

....

No. 304 Two childhood friends:

1. ....

2. ....

- Do you know what they're doing now?

1. ....

2. ....

CHILDHOOD MEMORIES

No. 305 Two books that influenced you as a child:

1. ....

2. ....

No. 306 A newspaper that was read in your home:

....

No. 307 A TV series you grew up with:

....

No. 308 A major worry during your childhood:

....

....

No. 309 A place where you felt safe?

....

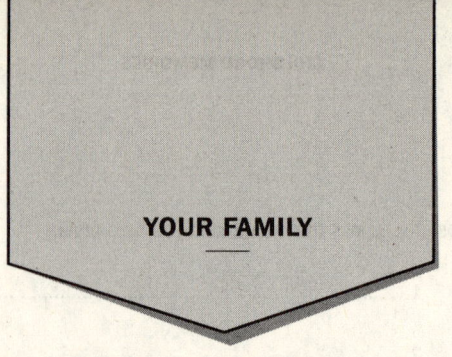

YOUR FAMILY

You know your family: some of these questions will apply to you, and some will need tweaking. Change any labels to fit your family best.

No. 310 Who do you feel closer to now: your mother or your father?

mother ←——————————→ father

No. 311 Who did you feel closer to as a child?

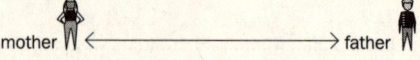

mother ←——————————→ father

No. 312 Who do you resemble more physically?

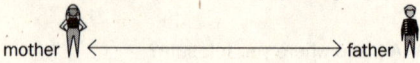

mother ←——————————→ father

No. 313 Something you like about your father:

....

YOUR FAMILY

No. 314 Something about your father that annoys you:

....

No. 315 A habit or characteristic you got from him:

....

No. 316 Describe your father in three words:

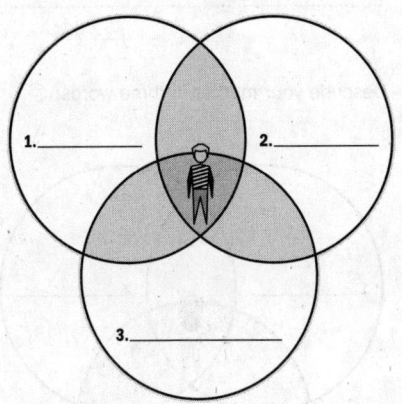

1. _____ 2. _____

3. _____

No. 317 How would your father describe you?

....

YOUR FAMILY

No. 318 Something you like about your mother:

....

No. 319 Something about your mother that annoys you:

....

No. 320 A habit or characteristic you got from her:

....

No. 321 Describe your mother in three words:

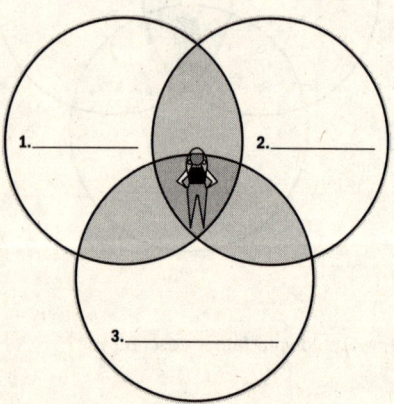

YOUR FAMILY

No. 322 How would your mother describe you?

....

No. 323 Are (or were) your parents happy together?

[ ] yes   [ ] no

No. 324 What do you admire your parents for?

....

• Why?

....

....

No. 325 What is one thing you wish your parents had done differently?

....

• Why?

....

....

YOUR FAMILY

No. 326 In what ways do you prefer your family to other families you know?

....

....

....

No. 327 Are your parents still alive?

[ ] yes   [ ] no   [ ] only one parent

• If no, is there something you wish you had said to them?

Father: ....

....

Mother: ....

....

• If yes, how often do you visit them?

[ ] several times a week   [ ] 2–5 times a month
[ ] 2–5 times a year   [ ] other

YOUR FAMILY

No. 328 If you grew up in a blended family ...

• What were the advantages?

....

....

....

• What were the disadvantages?

....

....

....

No. 329 Your favourite relatives:

• as a child: ....

• today: ....

No. 330 Describe the grandparent who you were (or are) closest to:

....

....

YOU AND YOUR SIBLINGS

	Sibling A
	....
No. 331 How are you alike?	
No. 332 How are you different?	
No. 333 What do you particuarly like about them?	
No. 334 What do you envy about them?	
No. 335 What would you like to tell them?	

YOU AND YOUR SIBLINGS

| Sibling B | Sibling C |
| .... | .... |

WHAT YOUR PARENTS THINK OF YOU

Ask your mother or father!
> If you can't or don't want to ask your parents, then ask yourself: how would they answer?

No. 336 Was I a difficult child?

....

....

No. 337 What did I most enjoy doing as a child?

....

....

....

No. 338 How well matched are my partner and I? Draw a cross on the line below:

not at all ⟵——————⟶ very well

WHAT YOUR PARENTS THINK OF YOU

No. 339 What worries you about me?

....

....

No. 340 What do you think about my chosen career?

....

....

No. 341 What about me makes you proud?

....

....

No. 342 Which of my character traits did I already have as a child?

....

....

....

....

LOVE

No. 343 Do you love your partner?

[ ] yes   [ ] no   [ ] don't know don't

- How can you tell?

....

....

....

No. 344 Does your partner love you?

[ ] yes   [ ] no   [ ] don't know

- How can you tell?

....

....

....

LOVE

No. 345 Do you feel desired?

[ ] yes   [ ] no

- Do you desire your partner?

[ ] yes   [ ] no

No. 346 Three things you value about your partner:

1. ....
2. ....
3. ....

No. 347 Three things you think your partner values about you:

1. ....
2. ....
3. ....

No. 348 What do you picture when you think about the love of your life?

....

No. 349 What do you think will be the greatest challenge in your relationship?

....

....

No. 350 What habit does your partner have that you need to learn to accept?

....

....

No. 351 Do you like your partner's friends?

[ ] yes   [ ] no

The ones you particularly like: ....

....

....

The ones you don't like at all: ....

....

....

No. 352 What bothers you about your partner's family?

....

....

No. 353 People tend to become more like their parents as they get older. Thinking of your partner, does this worry you?

[ ] yes   [ ] no

No. 354 In which situations do you feel or have you felt alienated from your partner?

....

....

No. 355 Do you like who you are in your partner's presence?

....

No. 356 Which of your weaknesses do you try to hide?

....

....

No. 357 How much do you earn compared with your partner?

[ ] more [ ] less [ ] about the same

No. 358 Something you can't talk to one another about:

....

....

....

No. 359 Would you want your partner to confess if they were unfaithful to you?

[ ] yes [ ] no

• Would you confess to your partner if you had been unfaithful?

[ ] yes [ ] no

• Have you agreed to do this?

[ ] yes [ ] no

• Does this mean you have been unfaithful?

[ ] yes [ ] no

LOVE

No. 360 What quality do you most wish your partner possessed?

....

No. 361 What quality do you think your partner most wishes you had?

....

No. 362 What do you miss most of what you've given up for your relationship?

....

....

....

No. 363 What makes your current partner different from your previous partners?

....

....

....

....

No. 364 Which of your previous partners can you imagine being in a relationship with again?

....

....

- Which can you imagine sleeping with again?

....

....

No. 365 Three characteristics you and your partner have in common:

1. ....

2. ....

3. ....

No. 366 Three ways in which you are different:

1. ....

2. ....

3. ....

No. 367 Which of the last two questions was easier to answer?

[ ] No. 365   [ ] No. 366

No. 368 How do you feel when your partner talks about his or her previous partner?

....

....

No. 369 How often do you have sex?

....

No. 370 Do your friends tend to advise you to separate or to stay together?

[ ] separate   [ ] stay together   [ ] neither

No. 371 Of the couples you know, which do you find the most unbearable?

....

No. 372 In relationships, have you more often been the one who left, or the one who was left?

[ ] I left them   [ ] I was left

- How do you explain that?

....

....

....

No. 373 If you're not married, would you like to be?

[ ] yes   [ ] no

- Why? ....

....

No. 374 What do you think is the most common myth about love?

....

....

....

LOVE

No. 375 Are you romantic?

[ ] yes [ ] no

- Why?

....

....

....

No. 376 Which song or piece of music do you associate with your relationship?

....

WHAT YOUR PARTNER THINKS OF YOU

Ask your partner or an ex-partner!
> If you don't want to or are unable to ask them, then ask yourself: how would my partner (or ex-partner) answer?

No. 377 What was I like when we first met?

....

....

....

....

No. 378 What am I like now?

....

....

....

....

No. 379 Two things about me you value:

1. ....

2. ....

No. 380 Two things about me that annoy you:

1. ....

2. ....

No. 381 In what situations have you felt disconnected from me?

....

....

....

No. 382 Something you learned from me:

....

....

....

BEING SINGLE

No. 383 When and to whom did you last say 'I love you'?

- When? ....

- To whom? ....

No. 384 When did someone last tell you they love you, and who was it?

- When? ....

- Who? ....

No. 385 How do you feel about being single?

....

No. 386 Approximately how many of your friends are single?

.... %

No. 387 For how much of your adult life have you been single?

....

- Why do you think that is?

....

....

No. 388 Your standard explanation about why you're not in a relationship:

....

....

....

No. 389 If you wanted a partner, what qualities would you look for?

....

....

....

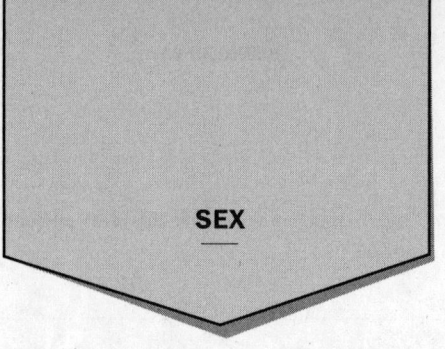

SEX

No. 390 What kind of person is usually attracted to you?

....

....

• What kind of person are you attracted to?

....

....

No. 391 A physical attribute that you are often complimented on:

....

No. 392 What intellectual characteristics do you find attractive?

....

....

SEX

No. 393 How many sexual partners have you had in your life?

[ ] 0–5   [ ] 6–10   [ ] 11–20
[ ] 21–40   [ ] 41–60   [ ] > 60

No. 394 Someone you regret having slept with:

....

No. 395 Someone you regret not having slept with:

....

No. 396 An unfulfilled sexual fantasy:

....

....

....

No. 397 A sexual fantasy that has been fulfilled:

....

....

....

No. 398 Someone you wanted and didn't get:

....

No. 399 Someone you wanted and did get:

....

No. 400 What are the pros of monogamy?

....

....

....

- And the cons?

....

....

....

No. 401 Which of your acquaintances are you sexually attracted to?

....

SEX

No. 402 Which of your close friends do you regard as a potential partner?

....

No. 403 How satisfying has your sex life been over the last three months?

not at all $\longleftarrow\longrightarrow$ very

No. 404 What is the longest you've gone without sex?

....

No. 405 How often do you masturbate?

....

YOUR FRIENDSHIPS

No. 406 Your longest-standing friendship:

....

No. 407 Your most unusual friendship:

....

No. 408 Describe your best friendship from your childhood:

....

....

....

No. 409 How are your current friendships different from your childhood friendships?

....

....

YOUR FRIENDSHIPS

No. 410 Your newest friendship:

....

No. 411 Your oldest friendship:

....

No. 412 The last argument you had with a friend:

....

....

- How did you resolve it?

....

....

No. 413 Have you ever ended a friendship with someone?

[ ] yes   [ ] no

- If yes, why? ....

- If no, why not? ....

YOUR FRIENDSHIPS

No. 414 Has anyone ever ended a friendship with you?

[ ] yes   [ ] no

- If yes, why? ....

- If no, why not? ....

No. 415 Describe a situation in which you have comforted someone:

....

....

....

- Who do you turn to when you need comforting?

....

- Who turns to you for comfort?

....

No. 416 Who do you most like to celebrate with?

....

YOUR FRIENDSHIPS

No. 417 Who is the most intelligent person you know?

....

No. 418 Do you have a friendship where you're more important to your friend than they are to you, and vice versa? Write their names.

- I am more important to them: ....

- They are more important to me: ....

No. 419 Which of your friends do you find attractive?

....

- Which of your partner's friends do you find attractive?

....

No. 420 Whose friendship could you do without?

....

- Why are you still nurturing it?

....

YOUR FRIENDSHIPS

No. 421 Is there someone you no longer see who you still think about?

....

No. 422 Who do you think knows you better than anyone else?

....

• Who do you know best?

....

No. 423 Have you ever hated anyone?

[ ] yes   [ ] no

• If yes, why and for how long?

....

....

No. 424 Who do you owe an apology to?

....

YOUR FRIENDSHIPS

No. 425 Describe a situation in which you've felt lonely:

....

....

No. 426 Add the names of five friends to the chart, showing how much happier or unhappier they are than you, and how much younger or older.

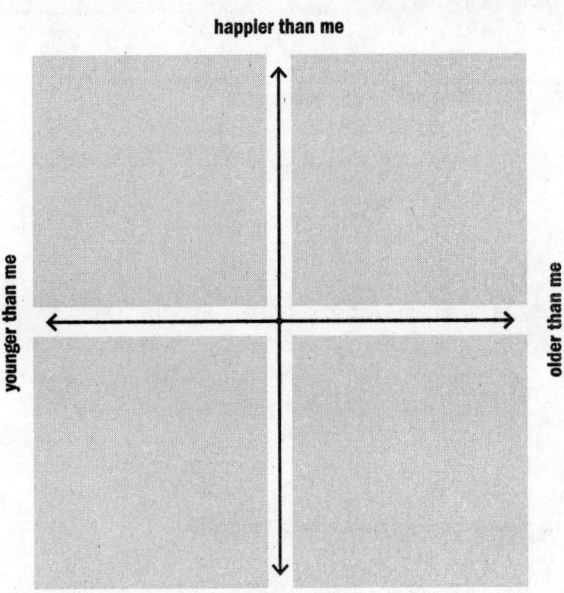

WHAT YOUR FRIENDS THINK OF YOU

Ask someone who knows you well!
If you don't want to or can't ask this person, ask yourself: how would they answer?

Name of the person: ....

No. 427 What am I really good at?

....

....

No. 428 What am I not so good at?

....

....

No. 429 Which profession would suit me?

....

WHAT YOUR FRIENDS THINK OF YOU

No. 430 What do I need to learn?

....

....

....

No. 431 Describe me in three words:

1. ....

2. ....

3. ....

No. 432 Rate me:

- How brave am I?

cowardly ⟵——————⟶ brave

- How reliable am I?

unreliable ⟵——————⟶ reliable

- How happy am I?

unhappy ⟵——————⟶ happy

YOUR FUTURE

No. 433 What will you be doing in ten years?

• Best-case scenario:

....

....

• Worst-case scenario:

....

....

No. 434 Who has an influence on your future?

....

No. 435 Whose future do you have an influence on?

....

YOUR FUTURE

No. 436 Which goal are you giving the most attention to right now?

....

• When do you want to have achieved this goal by?

....

• Will you succeed?   [ ] yes   [ ] no

No. 437 What would you like to master?

....

....

....

No. 438 Complete the sentences:

• If I had more time, I would ...

....

• If I had less time, I would ...

....

YOUR FUTURE

No. 439 Do you have a lifelong dream?

....

....

....

....

No. 440 Have you ever had your fortune told?

[ ] yes   [ ] no

- If so, did any of it come true?

[ ] yes   [ ] no

- If yes, what? ....

....

....

....

MAKING DECISIONS

No. 441 What do you make decisions with?

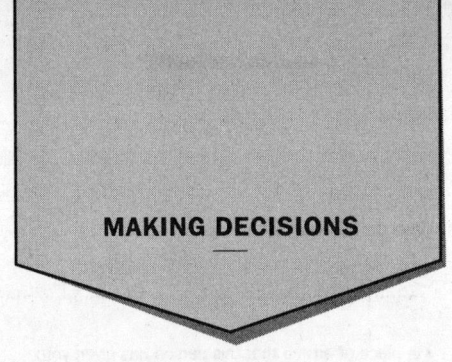

Head _____ %

Heart _____ %

Gut _____ %

Libido _____ %

No. 442 A typical situation in which you struggle to make a decision:

....

....

....

MAKING DECISIONS

No. 443 Who do you ask for advice?

....

- A piece of advice that this person has given you:

....

....

No. 444 Who asks you for advice?

....

No. 445 Is there a decision you've been putting off for a long time?

[ ] yes   [ ] no

- If yes, what is it?

....

- Why have you not managed to make that decision?

....

....

....

MAKING DECISIONS

No. 446 What was the best decision you made in the last five years?

....

....

- And the worst?

....

....

No. 447 How often do you keep your resolutions?

- In your career:

[ ] always [ ] often [ ] sometimes [ ] never

- In your relationship with your partner:

[ ] always [ ] often [ ] sometimes [ ] never

- In raising your children:

[ ] always [ ] often [ ] sometimes [ ] never

- In terms of your health:

[ ] always [ ] often [ ] sometimes [ ] never

THINKING ABOUT HAVING CHILDREN

No. 448 Do you like children?

[ ] yes   [ ] no

• Do children like you?

[ ] yes   [ ] no

• Do you want children? If so, how many?

....

No. 449 What's your biggest concern when you think about your own children?

....

No. 450 Would you rather have a boy or a girl? Explain why.

....

....

No. 451 Do you know how your partner acts around children?

[ ] yes   [ ] no

• Do you think your partner would be a good parent?

[ ] yes   [ ] no

No. 452 Do you know your partner's religious or spiritual beliefs?

[ ] yes   [ ] no

• Do you agree on how you would raise your children in this respect?

[ ] yes   [ ] no

No. 453 Have you discussed how you will share caring responsibilities for your children?

[ ] yes   [ ] no

No. 454 Would you adopt?

[ ] yes   [ ] no

No. 455 Would you consider IVF?

[ ] yes   [ ] no

No. 456 How do you feel about the idea of not having children?

....

....

No. 457 What reasons do you give when asked why you don't (yet) have children:

....

....

No. 458 Which parents do you see as role models?

....

....

BEING A PARENT

No. 459 What arguments are there for having children?

....

- And against having them?

....

No. 460 Something you never dared do, but which you hope your children will do:

....

....

No. 461 Something you have done and would advise your children against:

....

....

No. 462 A piece of advice that you received and followed as a child:

....

....

No. 463 What advice would you give your children about …

Relationships:

Career:

Friendship:

No. 464 What do you wish you had done differently with your children?

....

....

....

BEING A PARENT

No. 465 How have you changed since you had children?

....

....

No. 466 How has your partner changed?

....

....

No. 467 How has your relationship changed?

....

....

No. 468 What do your children think your job is?

....

....

No. 469 Do you have a favourite child?

[ ] no   [ ] yes ....

No. 470 If you are a grandparent: Do you feel that your children are bringing your grandchildren up well?

[ ] yes   [ ] no

• What are your children doing differently to you?

....

....

....

....

No. 471 If you are a grandparent: What would you like to pass on to your grandchildren?

....

....

....

....

ON HAPPINESS

No. 472 Is there anything stopping you from being happy? If so, what is it?

....

....

No. 473 What advice about being happy would you give?

....

....

No. 474 What are you looking forward to?

Today: ....

....

Every day: ....

....

No. 475 What are you happy to have left behind?

....

No. 476 What makes you unhappy?

....

No. 477 Something you typically do when you are...

- unhappy:

....

- happy:

....

No. 478 Someone you have made happy:

....

No. 479 Someone who has made you happy:

....

ON HAPPINESS

No. 480 A moment in which you were completely happy:

....

....

....

....

....

No. 481 Who is the happier of each pair?

    [ ] mother   [ ] father

    [ ] me   [ ] partner

    [ ] me   [ ] ex-partner

    [ ] me   [ ] best friend

    [ ] me today   [ ] me five years ago

A QUESTION OF FAITH

No. 482 Something you believe in, even though you can't prove its existence:

....

....

No. 483 Somewhere you go to find strength:

....

No. 484 How spiritual are you? Draw a cross on the line below:

not spiritual ⟵—————⟶ very spiritual

No. 485 What does 'being spiritual' mean to you?

....

....

....

A QUESTION OF FAITH

No. 486 What is your star sign?

....

• What does it say about you?

....

....

• Do you agree with it?

[ ] yes   [ ] no

[ ] yes, except for ....

....

No. 487 What do you no longer believe in that you believed ten years ago?

....

....

No. 488 What are your biggest doubts at the moment?

....

....

ONLY FOR BELIEVERS

A QUESTION OF FAITH

No. 489 How did you find your faith?

....

....

No. 490 If your religion involves prayer, how often do you pray and in which situations?

....

....

No. 491 What is your religion, and what drew you to it?

....

....

No. 492 Describe a situation that shook your belief:

....

No. 493 What, specifically, do you believe in?

....

....

A QUESTION OF FAITH

ONLY FOR NON-BELIEVERS

No. 494 Is there anything specifically that puts you off religion, or the idea that there could be a God/gods?

....

....

No. 495 Were you previously a believer but have lost your faith?

[ ] yes [ ] no

No. 496 How would you describe your view on existence?

....

....

No. 497 If you were to choose a religion, which would you pick?

....

No. 498 If you don't believe in God, what do you believe in?

....

....

No. 499 Who or what do you think you were in a former life?

....

No. 500 Do you believe in ...

• eternal love	[ ] yes	[ ] no
• life after death	[ ] yes	[ ] no
• fate	[ ] yes	[ ] no
• evolutionary theory	[ ] yes	[ ] no
• the self-regulating mechanisms of the free market	[ ] yes	[ ] no
• psychoanalysis	[ ] yes	[ ] no
• astrology	[ ] yes	[ ] no

YOUR FEARS

No. 501 What are you afraid of?

....

....

No. 502 What are you no longer afraid of?

....

....

No. 503 A recurring nightmare:

....

....

No. 504 Which illness scares you most?

....

YOUR FEARS

No. 505 Describe the most dangerous situation you've ever been in:

....

....

....

No. 506 What was the most difficult phase of your life?

....

....

....

- How did you get through it?

....

....

....

- Are you afraid of going through something like that again?

[ ] yes   [ ] no

YOUR FEARS

No. 507 Are you afraid of getting older? Of what in particular?

....

....

- Or are you looking forward to it? To what in particular?

....

....

No. 508 What do you think older people are better at than younger people?

....

....

No. 509 When was the last time you did something for the first time?

....

....

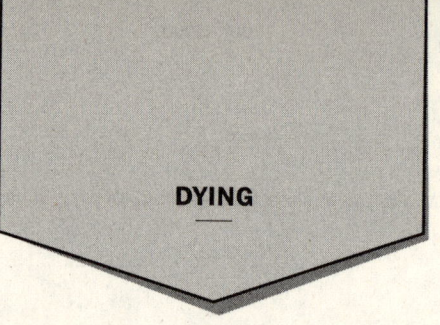

DYING

No. 510 When did you last go to a funeral?

....

No. 511 Think of loved ones who have died. Who comes to mind first?

....

No. 512 Of your friends or family, who do you fear might die next?

....

No. 513 If you found out that you had only a year left to live, would you change anything about your way of life?

[ ] yes   [ ] no

• If yes, what? ....

....

No. 514 Imagine that you're on your deathbed. Who would you like to say something to?

....

- What would you say to them?

....

....

....

- Why have you not already told them?

....

....

....

No. 515 Is there anything so important to you that life wouldn't be worth living without it? If so, what?

....

No. 516 What would you like to happen to your body after you die?

....

No. 517 Three words that you would like to be on your gravestone:

FINAL QUESTIONS

No. 518 Is now the best time of your life?

• If yes, why?

....

....

• If not, why not?

....

....

No. 519 Have you found your place in life?

• If yes, where is it?

....

No. 520 Are you a good friend?

[ ] yes   [ ] no

FINAL QUESTIONS

No. 521 What do you know how to do?

....

....

....

No. 522 Can you do all the things you want to be able to do?

....

....

....

No. 523 Are you happy with what you can do?

....

....

....

No. 524 What do you want to be able to do?

....

....

FINAL QUESTIONS

No. 525 How high are your energy levels?

No. 526 What percentage of your time do you spend living in the past, in the present and in the future (adding up to 100%)?

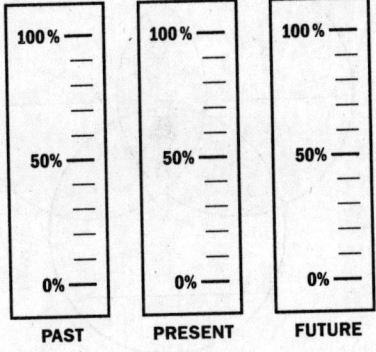

FINAL QUESTIONS

No. 527 Think about your career path. Mark on the career ladder:

- Where you are (A)

- Where you want to get (B)

- The highest rung you've ever reached (C)

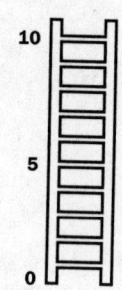

No. 528 Describe yourself in three words:

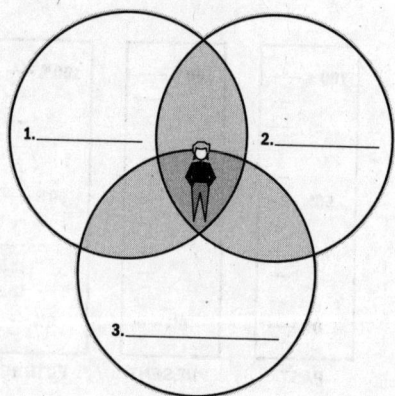

1. _____
2. _____
3. _____

FINAL QUESTIONS

No. 529 Without worrying about your artistic skills, draw something that represents you (an animal, a symbol, a number, etc.).

FINAL QUESTIONS

No. 530 When did you last cry?

....

- What was it about?

....

No. 531 When was the last time you belly laughed?

....

- Who were you with?

....

No. 532 What question do you ask yourself in life over and over?

....

- What is your answer right now?

....

....

YOUR QUESTIONS

YOUR QUESTIONS

YOUR QUESTIONS

YOUR QUESTIONS

YOUR QUESTIONS

YOUR QUESTIONS

YOUR QUESTIONS

YOUR QUESTIONS

YOUR QUESTIONS

YOUR QUESTIONS

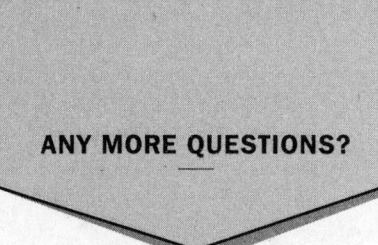

ANY MORE QUESTIONS?

This book has come to an end, but it isn't over. Which questions do you feel were missing? Can you think of other, better questions? Do you think we've ignored certain topics? Which questions have stuck in your mind? Do you have a particularly original answer to one of the questions?

If you have a question for us, or just want to get a comment off your chest, drop us a line. You'll find our contact details at www.rtmk.ch

ACKNOWLEDGEMENTS

This book only exists because of the generous support of a number of people.

It was read and tested by Simon Baumann, Dr Eugen Häni, Marlène Iseli, Miriam Lenz, Jörg Scholz, Solveig Scholz; the smartest questions came from Daniel Häni, Michael Krobath, Rebecca Lämmle, Franziska Schutzbach; the initial ideas from Andrea Schmidt; the best ideas from Annamateur, Dag Grödal, Facebook, Ondine Riesen; ruthless criticism from Senem Wicki; clichés were removed by Kenneth Domfe; and the most glaring mistakes were corrected by Andreas 'Becks' Dietrich.

ABOUT THE AUTHORS

MIKAEL KROGERUS

Three films that had a formative influence on me: *The Rescuers*, *In the Mood for Love*, *The Celebration*.

Three books I love: *Unknown Soldiers*, Väinö Linna; *Blood Meridian*, Cormac McCarthy; *Finn Family Moomintroll*, Tove Jansson.

Three things that annoy me in other people: holding grudges, competitiveness, lack of humour.

ROMAN TSCHÄPPELER

Three music albums that had a formative influence on me: *Back in Black*, AC/DC; *Engelberg*, Stephan Eicher; *Life on Planet Groove*, Maceo Parker.

Three of my current favourite topics of conversation: tennis, ski lifts, the future.

Three places I've lived: Biel/Bienne, Valencia, Aarhus.

Mikael Krogerus and Roman Tschäppeler are both graduates of the Kaospilot business school in Denmark. They are also the authors of the internationally bestselling series 'Little Books for Big Questions', which includes *The Decision Book*, *The Change Book*, *The Test Book*, *The Get Things Done Book* and *The Collaboration Book*. These books have been translated into more than 25 languages and have sold millions of copies.

www.rtmk.ch

This revised and updated edition published in 2024

First published in Great Britain in 2012 by
Profile Books Ltd
29 Cloth Fair
London
EC1A 7JQ
www.profilebooks.com

Copyright © 2021 for the new edition by Kein & Aber AG Zurich – Berlin. All rights reserved. The original version was published in 2009 under the title *Das Fragebuch* by Kein & Aber.

English-language translation copyright © Jamie Lee Searle 2024

10 9 8 7 6 5 4 3 2 1

Printed and bound in India by Manipal Technologies Limited

The moral right of the authors has been asserted.

All rights reserved. Without limiting the rights under copyright reserved above, no part of this publication may be reproduced, stored or introduced into a retrieval system, or transmitted, in any form or by any means (electronic, mechanical, photocopying, recording or otherwise), without the prior written permission of both the copyright owner and the publisher of this book.

A CIP catalogue record for this book is available from the British Library.

ISBN 978 1 80081 685 5
eISBN 978 1 80081 891 0